Presidential hypocrisy

Knowing that the past leaders in the free world had made

mistakes and are human

Every time, I hear and look at a president, it gives the impression that they are someone who should be looked up to, or be put on a pedestal for their accomplishments. Unfortunately every president are imperfect. Let's see in this book how some of these past presidents' lives really are and how imperfect they were despite leading one of the greatest countries in the world.

1. George Washington 1732-1799

First president of the United States (1789-1797)

Commander of armed forces for the Continental congress (1776-1783)

George was admired for his fearlessness in war as well as for his leadership abilities, but unfortunately the hypocrisy with George was that he owns slaves and while this does not look good for scholars, and people today, back in the 18th century, it was the way of life, unfortunately. George did leave in his will to set his slaves free after he and Martha Washington dies.

George

2.Thomas Jefferson 1743-1826

Author of the declaration of independence in 1776

US first secretary of state 1789-1793

Us Vice president 1797-1801

Thomas Jefferson believed that all men are created equal. He also believed that slavery was wrong. Unfortunately, Thomas was a hypocrite in more ways than one. He not only had slaves, he likely slept with one , His half-sister ,Sally hemings,Thomas Jefferson ,through biological testing , had several children with Sally Hemmings.

Thomas

3.James Madison (1751-1836)

Fourth president of the United states (1809 -1817)

Father of the United states Constitution (1787)

Secretary of state (1801-1809)

James Madison was a very wise man when he quoted to his fellow countrymen that "Men are not angels and if men were, we would not need a constitution to help govern the country"; Despite James Madison's brilliance as a founding father and statesman .He was also a slave owner which illustrates the hypocrisy and duality that human beings faced every day.

James Madison picture

James

4.James Monroe 1758-1831

Fifth president of the United States

1817-1825

Congressman

Secretary of war, state (1817-1825)

James Monroe was a great statesman, and whom, during his presidency ,helped develop a landmark policy called the "Monroe doctrine ".Unfortunately The hypocrisy with him was that he was a slave owner yet he did wanted slaves to be free

James Monroe

5.Andrew Jackson 1767-1845

7th president of the United States (1829-1837)

Andrew Jackson was a very popular president for his time, his election in 1828 mark the beginning of time where the spoils system began and he also paid off the national debt. The hypocrisy with Andrew was that he was a slave owner; believe in white supremacy, white suffrage and his involvement in the trail of tears. His notorious reputation is so tarnished by his racism and involvement in the forcing of Indians into marked territories in the west despite the US Supreme Court acknowledgement that the trail of tears or Indian removal policy was unconstitutional

uncommitted to any other course than the strict line of constitutional duty; and that the securities for this independence may be rendered as strong as the nature of power and the weakness of its possessor will admit. — I cannot too earnestly invite your attention to the propriety of promoting such an amendment of the constitution as will render him ineligible after one term of service.

It gives me pleasure to announce to Congress that the benevolent policy of the Government, steadily pursued for nearly thirty years in relation to the removal of the Indians beyond the white settlements, is approaching to a happy consummation. Two important tribes have accepted the provision made for their removal at the last session of Congress; and it is believed that their example will induce the remaining tribes, also, to seek the same obvious advantages.

The consequences of a speedy removal will be important to the United States, to individual States, and to the Indians themselves. The pecuniary advantages which it promises to the Government, are the least of its recommendations. It puts an end to all possible danger of

Writings by Andrew Jackson to congress to support the removal of Indians from south USA

6.Andrew Johnson

17th president 1869-1877

Andrew Johnson was a southerner; he was elected vice president under Abraham Lincoln, unfortunately, after Abraham Lincoln was assassinated on April 14, 1865. He became President, yet his truly hypocritical moment was despite being the vice president to a president who was determined to help the freedmen gain legal citizen status to the reconstruction, as president, his white supremacist views of African Americans had led to the demise of reconstruction, paving the way for 100 more years of oppression and suffering for many African Americans at that time.

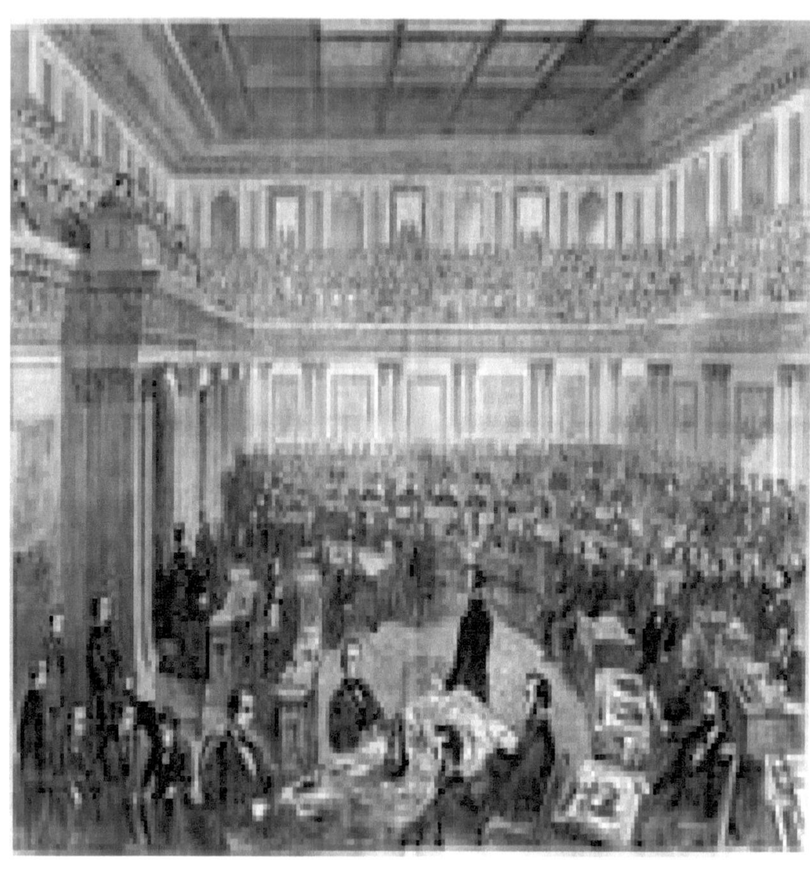

Andrew Johnson’s impeachment trial

In 1867, 1868

7.Theodore Roosevelt 1856-1919

1901-1909

While Theodore continues to be seen as one of America's greatest presidents; however he did things that were unjust thus hypocritical to the office of the presidency

Theodore Roosevelt 's presidential hypocrisy was the Brownville raid in which he honorably discharged several negro soldiers called the buffalo soldiers who were wrongly accused of killing two white men despite the military commanders and supervisors admission that the soldiers were all in their beds that night .There was evidence that was plotted against the negro buffalo soldiers . Roosevelt gave his the orders stemming from an inspector general's investigation. Other violations Roosevelt committed were the alleged corruption in getting the Panama Canal installed in 1903.

Theodore Roosevelt

8.Woodrow Wilson 1856-1924

28th president of the United states 1913-1921

Woodrow Wilson was and still is the only past president who obtained a PHD. Woodrow Wilson is considered by historians to be a great president due to his leadership during World War I and his quest to create the League of Nations .While his ideas for the League of Nations did not happen during his presidency or in his lifetime. His idea was the blue print for the eventual formation of the United Nations. Woodrow Wilson was a scholar, whose ideas about government during his tenure as Governor of Virginia led to the forming of Public administration as a business.

However Woodrow Wilson's racism, his inconspicuous beliefs regarding segregation had shown that he was a hypocrite which has now tarnished his legacy 100 years later.

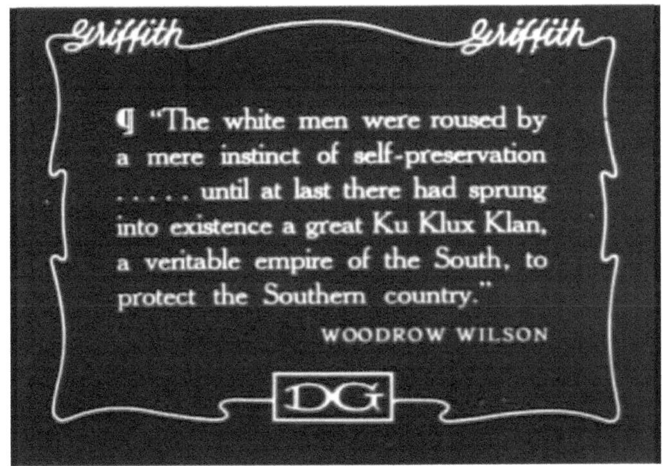

Woodrow Wilson's history of the American people was quoted in the "birth of a nation" movie" which shown the Ku Klux Klan as a strong force. The movie also shown direct racism as its message was that integration was wrong, African Americans were not equal and Reconstruction was a disaster for the country. Other racist policies committed by Wilson were enforcing segregation in the military forces and in the United States government; He also had the "birth of a nation" movie screened in the White house in 1915. It was the first motion picture screened in the white house. Woodrow Wilson was a white supremacist who believed that segregation was a benefit for African American men. It was during his tenure as the Princeton University President, he refused to accept any black students and he dismissed lynchings as a lawless reaction to a lawless period. This hypocrisy shows Woodrow Wilson to be a true racist for his time.

Woodrow Wilson.

9.Warren G Harding 1921—1923

Warren G Harding was a very popular president for his time, however his hypocrisy was his contradiction in not getting a federal anti-lynching bill passed,in 1922. The other reasons includes the numerous scandals in his administration such as the teapot dome and the Veterans Bureau controversies.The revelation regarding the extramarital affairs he had with Carrie Fulton Phillips before he was president and his other mistress ,Nan Britton who claims that one of her children was fathered by Harding.

A DNA test conducted in the year 2015 genetically proved that Harding did father his mistress's daughter.

Warren G Harding

Albert Fall, was Warren G Harding 's secretary of interior, He went to prison for his involvement in the Teapot scandal due to his involvement in illegal bribes involving the hiring of his friends for leases with the naval bases near Teapot Wyoming . He was found guilty of conspiracy and bribery and he was sent to jail for one year

10.Presidential scandals are the obvious form of hypocrisy and here are some slogans

"All the News That's Fit to Print"

The New York Times

LATE CITY EDITION

Weather: Partly cloudy today; cool tonight. Fair, pleasant tomorrow. Temp. range: today 63-78; Thursday 64-85. Highest Temp.-Hum. Index yesterday: 73. Details on Page 66.

VOL. CXXIII..No. 42,566 — NEW YORK, FRIDAY, AUGUST 9, 1974 — 15 CENTS

NIXON RESIGNS

HE URGES A TIME OF 'HEALING'; FORD WILL TAKE OFFICE TODAY

'Sacrifice' Is Praised; Kissinger to Remain

By ANTHONY RIPLEY

WASHINGTON, Aug. 8—Vice President Ford praised President Nixon tonight for "one of the greatest personal sacrifices for the country and one of the finest personal decisions on behalf of all of us as Americans."

Mr. Ford, who will take office as the 38th President at noon tomorrow, vowed to continue Mr. Nixon's foreign policy and announced that Secretary of State Kissinger had agreed to stay on in the new Administration.

"I pledge to you tonight, as I will pledge to you tomorrow and in the future, my best efforts in cooperation, leadership and dedication to what's good for America and good for the world," he said.

The Vice President, who never sought the nation's highest office and disclaimed any intention of seeking it after Mr. Nixon's term, will take the oath of office in a private ceremony at the White House.

Thus will he become the first man to serve as President without being chosen by the American people in an election. Tomorrow night he will address the nation on radio and television. It is expected that he will speak at 6 P.M.

All day today the signs of the historic change were in the air, sensed by the crowds that gathered along Pennsylvania

Text of Mr. Ford's remarks appears on Page 2.

Avenue near the White House. Applause rang out from the crowds when Mr. Ford appeared briefly.

After watching Mr. Nixon on television tonight with his family, the Vice President stepped outside into a slight drizzle at his suburban split-level home in nearby Alexandria, Va., to face television cameras and

SPECULATION RIFE ON VICE PRESIDENT

Some Ford Associates Say Selecting a Successor Could Take Weeks

By CHRISTOPHER LYDON

WASHINGTON, Aug. 8 — Potentially the most revealing and most important decision of Gerald R. Ford's Presidential debut — his choice of a successor in the Vice Presidency —

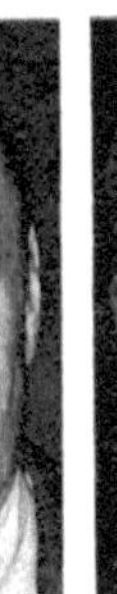

Vice President Ford meeting with newsmen last night

President Nixon on TV as he announced his resignation

The 37th President Is First to Quit Post

By JOHN HERBERS

WASHINGTON, Aug. 8—Richard Milhous Nixon, the 37th President of the United States, announced tonight that he had given up his long and arduous fight to remain in office and would resign, effective at noon tomorrow.

At that hour, Gerald Rudolph Ford, whom Mr. Nixon nominated for Vice President last Oct. 12, will be sworn in as the 38th President, to serve out the 895 days remaining in Mr. Nixon's second term.

Less that two years after his landslide re-election victory, Mr. Nixon, in a conciliatory address on national

Text of the address will be found on Page 2.

television, said that he was leaving not with a sense of bitterness but with a hope that his departure would start a "process of healing that is so desperately needed in America."

He spoke of regret for any "injuries" done "in the course of the events that led to this decision." He acknowledged that some of his judgments had been wrong.

The 61-year-old Mr. Nixon, appearing calm and resigned to his fate as a victim of the Watergate scandal, became the first President in the history of the Republic to resign from office. Only 10 months earlier Spiro Agnew resigned the Vice-Presidency.

Speaks of Pain at Yielding Post

Mr. Nixon, speaking from the Oval Office, where his successor will be sworn in tomorrow, may well have delivered his most effective speech since the Watergate scandals began to swamp his Administration in early 1973.

In tone and content, the 15-minute address was in sharp contrast to his frequently combative language of the past, especially his first "farewell" appearance—that of 1962, when he announced he was retiring from politics after losing the

POLITICAL SCENE SHARPLY ALTERED

G.O.P. Prospects Improved, Ford in Good Spot for '76 and Watergate Fades

By R. W. APPLE Jr.

Rise and Fall
Appraisal of Nixon Career

By ROBERT B. SEMPLE Jr.

The central question is how a man who won so much could have lost so much. How could a public figure who so well perceived the instincts of the majority of his countrymen have misused the powers and duties and who, on reaching his destination, was not always certain what to do when he got there—except, perhaps, to keep going.

That image has only been re-

JAWORSKI ASSERTS NO DEAL WAS MADE

Says Nixon Did Not Ask for and Was Not Given a Way to Avoid Prosecution

By RICHARD D. LYONS

The Watergate scandal, the cover-up which led to Richard Nixon's resignation in 1974, Richard Nixon (1969-1974), the 37th president was tarnished for his involvement in the Watergate affair

The Lewinsky scandal which led to the impeachment hearings of Bill Clinton was big news and even though it did not have anything to do with Bill Clinton's presidential actions. The some members of the public at the time of the scandal in 1998 viewed it as a violation and therefore, it could be a possible action of hypocrisy. Despite the scandal Bill Clinton was a very popular president at the time of the controversial event. His post presidency actions and the eventual candidacy of his wife, Hillary Rodham Clinton for president in 2016 improve his presidential standing and legacy among historians

Ulysses S Grant had many scandals in his administration. There was the Whiskey Ring, and the Credit Mobiler scandals, Ulysses S Grant 1868-1877, the 18th president was seen as very corrupt as many members of his administration were involved in bribery and corruption

11.John Kennedy 1917-1963

35th president of United States

1961-1963

Some would say John F Kennedy's numerous extramarital affairs show hypocrisy. I declined to write about it because his personal life was not a target during his administration .However his personal involvement with numerous mistresses does show a degree of hypocrisy at least in character.

john

John Kennedy and his alleged mistress ,actress Marilyn Monroe in 1962

Ronald

12.Ronald Reagan (1911-2004)

The 40th president of the United States

1981 -1989

President Reagan's actions as president during the cold war, and his charisma made him one of the most popular presidents in history; unfortunately, with each president presumably there were some flaws. The hypocrisy in his presidential actions was shown by the Iran contra affair in 1987, when several members of his administration facilitated giving secret arms to Iran, despite the laws forbidding a sales embargo. Another big flaw was his refusal to get his administration help people suffering from the Aids virus which led to thousands of people dying and the delay of funding for medications to people diagnosed with hive, the virus that causes aids

12.Donald Trump 2017-

Donald trump have so much hypocrisy that It is numerous to describe. His laten bigotry towards immigrants during the 2016 election, His racist background as his father was a white supremacist allegedly and his laten beliefs toward white supremacy, Donald Trump is the true testament to presidential imperfection and hypocrisy.

The picture above of the "Donald" and below is evidence that his father Fred trump was arrested fighting the cops during a Ku Klux Klan rally in 1927 which leads to speculation that his father was a white supremacist

SCENE AS POLICE AND KLAN CLASH IN QUEENS PARADE

Scene on Queens blvd., where police tried to turn Klansmen out of Memorial Day parade. Officer at left is about to swing his night-stick over the head of white-sheeted knight, whose friends rushed to assist, causing a free-for-all with two auto loads of policemen.

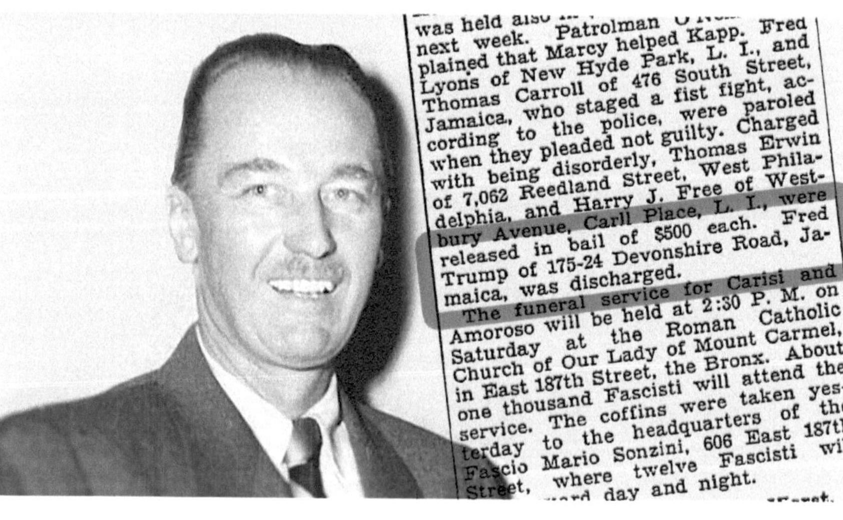

was held also ... Patrolman O'N...
next week. Fred
plained that Marcy helped Kapp.
Lyons of New Hyde Park, L. I., and
Thomas Carroll of 476 South Street,
Jamaica, who staged a fist fight, according to the police, were paroled
when they pleaded not guilty. Charged
with being disorderly, Thomas Erwin
of 7,062 Reedland Street, West Phila-
delphia, and Harry J. Free of West-
bury Avenue, Carll Place, L. I., were
released in bail of $500 each. Fred
Trump of 175-24 Devonshire Road, Jamaica, was discharged.

The funeral service for Carisi and
Amoroso will be held at 2:30 P. M. on
Saturday at the Roman Catholic
Church of Our Lady of Mount Carmel,
in East 187th Street, the Bronx. About
one thousand Fascisti will attend the
service. The coffins were taken yesterday to the headquarters of the
Fascio Mario Sonzini, 606 East 187th
Street, where twelve Fascisti wi...
...ard day and night.

TWO FASCISTI DIE IN BRONX, KLANSMEN RIOT IN QUEENS, IN MEMORIAL DAY CLASHES

SLAIN ON WAY TO PARADE

One Man Is Stabbed and Another Shot—Their Assailants Escape.

FIST FIGHTS IN JAMAICA

Police Battle Hooded Klansmen When They Refuse to Leave Pageant.

100 Sheep, a Camel and Rugs Sacrificed at Rail Opening

CONSTANTINOPLE, May 30 (AP).—The traditional sacrifice of 100 sheep, with the innovation of a huge camel, laden with costly rugs and brilliant shawls, was made today by the townsfolk of Caesarea on the occasion of the opening of the 240-mile Angora Caesarea railway.

The railway, carrying modernity further to the east in Turkey, represents the first achievement of the republic's vast rail building program and is the first line completed entirely by the Turks.

The first train carried Premier Ismet Pasha, who officiated at the inauguration during which the sacrifice of the camel and sheep took place.

The Justice Department sued his company — twice — for not renting to black people

When Trump was serving as the president of his family's real estate company, the Trump Management Corporation, in 1973, the Justice Department sued the company for alleged racial discrimination against black people looking to rent apartments in Brooklyn, Queens and Staten Island.

The lawsuit charged that the company quoted different rental terms and conditions to black rental candidates than it did with white candidates, and that the company lied to black applicants about apartments not being available. Trump called those accusations "absolutely ridiculous" and sued the Justice Department for $100 million in damages for defamation.

Without admitting wrongdoing, the Trump Management Corporation settled the original lawsuit two years later and promised not to discriminate against black people, Puerto Ricans or other minorities. Trump also agreed to send weekly vacancy lists for his 15,000 apartments to the New York Urban League, a civil rights group, and to allow the NYUL to present qualified applicants for vacancies in certain Trump properties.

Just three years after that, the Justice Department sued the Trump Management Corporation again for allegedly discriminating against black applicants by telling them apartments weren't available.

In fact, discrimination against black people has been a pattern in his career

Workers at Trump's casinos in Atlantic City, New Jersey, have accused him of racism over the years. The New Jersey Casino Control Commission fined the Trump Plaza Hotel and Casino $200,000 in 1992 because managers would remove African-American card dealers at the request of a certain big-spending gambler. A state appeals court upheld the fine.

The first-person account of at least one black Trump casino employee in Atlantic City suggests the racist practices were consistent with Trump's personal behavior toward black workers.

"When Donald and Ivana came to the casino, the bosses would order all the black people off the floor," Kip Brown, a former employee at Trump's Castle, told the New Yorker for a September article. "It was the eighties, I was a teen-ager, but I remember it: they put us all in the back."

Trump disparaged his black casino employees as "lazy" in vividly bigoted terms, according to a 1991 book by John O'Donnell, a former president of Trump Plaza Hotel and Casino.

"And isn't it funny. I've got black accountants at Trump Castle and Trump Plaza. Black guys counting my money! I hate it," O'Donnell recalled Trump saying. "The only kind of people I want counting my money are short guys that wear yarmulkes every day."

"I think the guy is lazy," Trump said of a black employee, according to O'Donnell. "And it's probably not his fault because laziness is a trait in blacks. It really is, I believe that. It's not anything they can control."

Trump has also faced charges of reneging on commitments to hire black people. In 1996, 20 African Americans in Indiana sued Trump for failing to honor a promise to hire mostly minority workers for a riverboat casino on Lake Michigan.

TAYLOR HILL/GETTY IMAGES

Apparently Sen. Jeff Sessions (R-Ala.) does not mind Trump's racism. Sessions endorsed the GOP front-runner on Monday.

He refused to condemn the white supremacists who are campaigning for him

Three times in a row on Feb. 28, Trump sidestepped opportunities to renounce white nationalist and former KKK leader David Duke, who told his radio audience last week that voting for any candidate other than Trump is "really treason to your heritage."

When asked by CNN's Jake Tapper if he would condemn Duke and say he didn't want a vote from him or any other white supremacists, Trump claimed that he didn't know anything about white supremacists or about Duke himself. When Tapper pressed him twice more, Trump said he couldn't condemn a group he hadn't yet researched.

By Feb. 29, Trump was saying that in fact he does disavow Duke, and that the only reason he didn't do so on CNN was because of a "lousy earpiece." Video of the exchange, however, shows Trump responding quickly to Tapper's questions with no apparent difficulty in hearing.

It's preposterous to think that Trump doesn't know about white supremacist groups or their sometimes violent support of him. Reports of neo-Nazi groups rallying around Trump go back as far as August.

His white supremacist fan club includes the Daily Stormer, a leading neo-Nazi news site; Richard Spencer, director of the National Policy Institute, which aims to promote the "heritage, identity, and future of European people"; Jared Taylor, editor of American Renaissance, a Virginia-based white nationalist magazine; Michael Hill, head of the League of the South, an Alabama-based white supremacist secessionist group; and Brad Griffin, a member of Hill's League of the South and author of the popular white supremacist blog Hunter Wallace.

A leader of the Virginia KKK who is backing Trump told a local TV reporter earlier this month, "The reason a lot of Klan members like Donald Trump is because a lot of what he believes, we believe in."

And most recently, the Trump campaign announced that one of its California primary delegates was William Johnson, chair of the white nationalist American Freedom Party. The Trump campaign subsequently said his inclusion was a mistake, and Johnson withdrew his name at their request.

www.ingramcontent.com/pod-product-compliance
Ingram Content Group UK Ltd.
Pitfield, Milton Keynes, MK11 3LW, UK
UKHW041832200726
13854UKWH00003BA/1108

9 781387 248285